Palmistry
Made Easy

Palmistry
Made Easy

Johnny Fincham

Winchester, UK
Washington, USA

First published by Dodona Books, 2012
Dodona Books is an imprint of John Hunt Publishing Ltd., Laurel House, Station Approach,
Alresford, Hants, SO24 9JH, UK
office1@jhpbooks.net
www.johnhuntpublishing.com

For distributor details and how to order please visit the 'Ordering' section on our website.

Text copyright: Johnny Fincham 2011

ISBN: 978 1 84694 620 2

A CIP catalogue record for this book is available from the British Library.

Design: Stuart Davies

Printed and bound by CPI Group (UK) Ltd, Croydon, CR0 4YY

We operate a distinctive and ethical publishing philosophy in all
areas of our business, from our global network of authors to
production and worldwide distribution.

CONTENTS

CHAPTER ONE

In the beginning...

Introduction

On the face of it, palmistry seems an outdated and outlandishly simplistic practice. The idea that one's character, strengths, weaknesses, life experiences and so on can be marked in our palms seems childish and irrational. Yet this is indeed the case as you will soon discover. Traditionally, palmistry has focused on the palm lines and made (rather fatalistic) predictions from them. This has resulted in a burden of fear, superstition and scepticism. However, it's in the broader aspects of palmistry: the relative length of the digits, the print patterns and so on, that science has come to verify and expand on much of traditional palmistry theory. Back in 1936, the physician and psychoanalyst, Charlotte Wolff identified distinct palm patterns on those with severe learning disorders. In much more recent times the anthropological researcher, John Manning has conducted experiments proving that certain finger length configurations indicate definite human characteristics.

Palmistry has never been more vibrant, progressive and powerful than now. In criminology, psychology, anthropology and genetics, the palm is proving to be an incredible mirror into the workings of the human mind.

As we begin this book, our first understanding has to be that far from being a fatalistic, determining art, palmistry is an instrument of personal liberation. While the palm does indicate the overall characteristics of a subject, the lines of the palm change over time, so nothing is fixed. Our lives are literally and figuratively in our own hands. It's the essential self-knowledge of our fundamental drives, fears, strengths and weaknesses that palmistry provides that makes it such a wondrous, illuminating art. With palmistry as your tool you can help yourself and others live more appropriate, more fulfilling and happier lives.

Wait a minute!

Palmistry is a relatively easy art to master if you have the patience to learn each point thoroughly. Impatience is the greatest obstacle to this jewel of knowledge. Make sure you've absorbed each point and see if you can find it in a hand or two, before you move on.

I recommend you approach the process with scepticism. Don't believe anything you see written here. Rather, try each point out on yourself, family and friends and see if it's valid or not. Let the proof of this ancient practice slowly reveal itself to you. For palmistry, if it is about anything, it's about truth. And we, as palmists, have a responsibility to be truthful to ourselves and our clients above all things.

Five Palmistry Golden rules

1 No one point should be taken as an indication of character. A human being is the sum of *all* the qualities of their palm.
2 We covet most what we lack. Those qualities which are missing in a person are those they value most highly.
3 The lines of the palm change over time.
4 There is a positive side to every marking.
5 People are extremely vulnerable when they offer you their palm to read. Never rush to make an observation, take your time, be gentle, be kind, but be honest.

Palm Printing

Before you learn the process of actually reading palms, it's essential to learn a practical skill - that of taking hand prints. Acquiring the knack of taking good quality prints is a key step in your hand-reading journey. When you read a palm from a print, you pick up much finer detail than you would if you just read the naked palm. Also, this allows you to look at the person's palm alone, without them watching you and pressing you to stun them with your insight. This makes learning the process much easier and less pressured. A further bonus is that the lineal changes that occur through time are easy to see if you take prints and compare them as the years go by.

You will need block printing, water-based ink; an ink roller (both available from arts and crafts shops) and plain A4 photocopying paper.

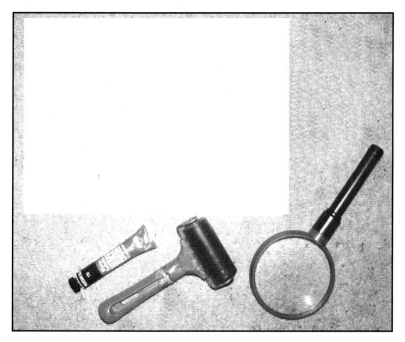

1. Equipment

Squeeze 1cm. of ink onto any smooth non-absorbent surface. Roll the ink (black or a dark colour is best) until the roller is covered. Try to use the minimum amount of ink. Roll the ink over the palm, covering the whole surface including the fingers with an even, thin layer. Clients tend to stretch out their palm while the ink is applied, but it's best to get them to relax their hands as much as possible. Follow the contours of the hand and retouch any bare patches.

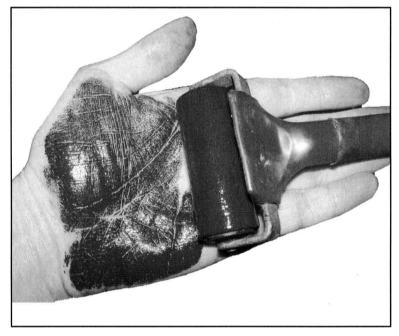

2. Inking the palm

Place a couple of magazines under the print paper and press the palm down onto the paper with firm pressure using both your own hands. Make sure you push down on the whole of the palm and fingers. Draw around the palm and fingers and lift the hand off carefully, hold the printed paper down with one hand while you do so.

When reading palms, the need for good light can't be over-emphasised. An illuminated magnifying glass is extremely useful; it doesn't need to be particularly high magnification. Callipers or dividers are useful for beginners to compare finger lengths.

There's a shorthand you can use to indicate various qualities of the palm that can't be ascertained from a print alone. Start drawing in the form of the dermatoglyphic patterns (the print patterns), add an arrow pointing up or down above each digit to indicate if a finger is longer or shorter than average. Handedness is illustrated with RH for right-handed or LH for a left-handed person. Stiffness of the fingers and thumbs is indicated by a number scale of 1 - 5 where five is floppy, three is average and one is rigidly immobile. Skin texture is indicated by writing the words 'silk', 'paper', 'grainy' or 'coarse'. If finger knots are well-developed this is noted. Write out the details of the thumb's length, stiffness and print pattern as the thumb tends to be side-on to the paper and prints poorly.

CHAPTER TWO

The Shape of things to come…

Hand and brain

The best way to view the palm is a window into the workings of the brain. In terms of anthropological development, there's a clearly established link between the way the human hand has become increasingly sophisticated and the way the human brain has evolved. A massive amount of the cerebral cortex is devoted to the palms. In proportion to the amount of brain surface area given to, for example, the knees, the palm's cortex area is for a pair of organs each around four square feet in size!

Take a look at these two palm prints. This lady has had a major, stress-induced psychological breakdown. The first print (3) shows her palm just at the point of the breakdown. The

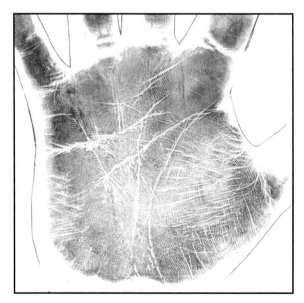

3. At point of breakdown

second (4) shows her hand four months later after a period of sustained rest and recuperation. Can there be any more telling evidence that the palms are the 'visible brain?'

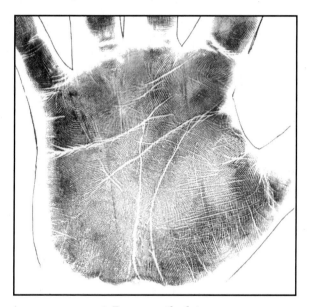

4. Four months later

Palm size

A word about palm size. Some people have disproportionately bigger or smaller palms than average in relation to body size. An easy way to check this is by comparing someone's hand to the size of their face. When the base of the palm is lined up with the chin, the fingertips should rest around the mid-forehead level.

Large hands

People with large palms are plodders. They take things slowly, they're pedantic, deliberate and like life on a small scale. Big hands are great with tiny details and they often work in fields that require meticulous care where the focus is on getting things just right: jewellery makers, dental technicians, classical musicians, painting restorers, research scientists. They can often

miss the bigger picture as they're so absorbed in the painstak-
ingly miniscule.

Small hands

Those with small palms are unconcerned with details and have
no time for the minutiae of life. They always see the bigger
picture and are firmly focused on the road ahead. Small handed
people are impatient and love to balance lots of plans and
projects at once, rushing to deal with things head-on. Small
palms are suited to working in busy environments and in taking
the initiative, but they'll always need someone to clear up and
dot the 'i's' behind them!

Active and passive

So, which hand do we examine? The right or the left?

Well, the answer is that any good palmist will examine both
palms, whether the person is right or left handed, old or young,
male or female. Traditionally the hand you use to write with (the
right on most of us) is termed the active hand while the one you
use less (usually, but not always the left) is called the passive
hand. The difference between the palms is that the active hand
shows the more surface, developed, expressive and outward
personality and the passive palm shows the deeper, latent,
hidden, personal and private personality. Both palms are
indicative of how you are now, but everyone has a deeper side of
their personality that's usually hidden. The active and passive
hands are like the difference between the person you know as a
working colleague, or acquaintance (active) and the person you
eventually come to know when you've lived with them for ten
years and know them intimately (passive).

The differences between the active and passive palms are the
key to knowing why a person acts as they do. There might be a
set of good, clear, strong lines showing an effective, balanced
person on the active palm, but that soul may be driven by all sorts

of inner demons you may discover in the form of distorted, fractured and broken lines on the passive hand. The lines on the passive hand show patterns that run deeper and that are more internalised. They show issues that go back to childhood.

Tempting though it is to jump straight to the palmer lines, it's essential to build up an understanding of character through the shape and form of the palm itself, the skin texture, the fingers and fingerprints. These essential stepping stones are the bedrock of modern palmistry. The lines are meaningless without reference to these points.

The form of the palm

The shape and form of the palm reflects the broad outline of the individual's cerebral cortex and shows which (if any) aspects are more developed. At this stage, we're at a fairly crude level of analysis and much more subtle indications will be examined later.

First of all, are the fingers long or short?

Short fingers

If they're short, the person's mental processes will be short and holistic. They like to be realistic, relative, and they calculate quickly with little time for details. They're multi-taskers with a 'hands on' approach. Check out the finger length of anyone that makes quick decisions - one of life's doers, you'll find they have short fingers.

The exception to this is when the digits have enlarged joints and are knotty. Knots tend to slow down and re-circulate the thought process. If someone's fingers have pronounced knots

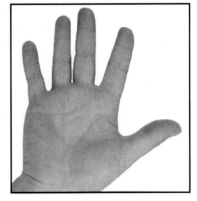

5. Short fingers

they'll be argumentative, pedantic and exacting. It makes for logical, detailed and thorough mental processes. Pronounced knots make it hard to be spontaneous.

Long fingers

Long-fingered people have long thoughts, they dwell on things mentally and take a long view. Long-fingered folk tend to be specialists, they like to think things over and have a good eye for detail. Look at the fingers of a classical musician or a researcher. Long-fingered people refine and assess information before they act.

6. Long fingers

The quadrants

Now let's check out the palm itself. The palm is split roughly into four quarters. Each quarter relates to a different aspect of human experience and of human psychology. It's helpful to know about these zones because later on, when we examine the lines and print patterns on the palm, we'll know what area of human concern they relate to.

These areas of the palm are particularly important if they're enlarged. This will exaggerate the zone's qualities in the person's mental process and affect their behaviour.

Let's start with the quadrant where the thumb attaches. Press your thumb into the ball of flesh there. This area is known as the primal Home, Body and Family quadrant. The larger and more muscular this zone, the more reserves of physical energy, the greater the lust for life and sense of human warmth. On a woman's palm, if this area is large and

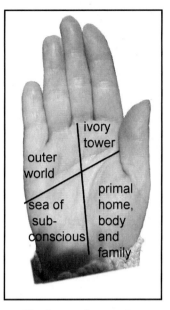

7. The four palm quadrants

muscular, it's likely she'll have a large family. Both genders with this quality will be physical, active people.

If the mount is soft and spongy, there's a residual sensuality, a love of food, leisure and luxury. Maintaining a strict diet can feel like torture.

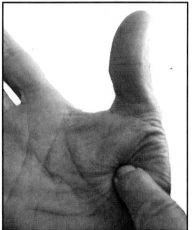

8. Spongy thumb ball

However, if this area is hard and flat without a pronounced mount, there's a Spartan quality. This is a person that can do without luxuries, soft cushions and life's pleasures; one that can easily resist that chocolate bar! They might lack a little in the human warmth department, though.

Sometimes there's an over-developed area lower down,

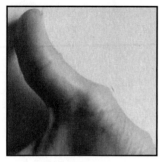

9. Pronounced lower thumb angle

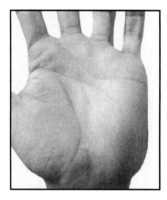

10. Enlarged Sea of Subconscious area

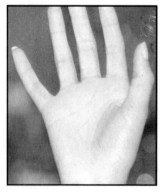

11. Enlarged Outer World area

beneath the thumb, where an angled, bony projection is clearly visible. This creates an ability to connect with the physical world with skill and precision. Also, there's a noticeable sense of rhythm. Everyone from engineers to artisans and dancers have this marking, there's a love of getting one's hands involved in something physical and developing some practical skill.

Opposite the primal Home, Body and Family quadrant in the lower part of the palm is the Sea of Subconscious area. If it's enlarged by bulging outward or upward, there's a love of the sea and of nature, the person is likely to be creative and imaginative, to love mystery and all things spiritual.

Above this is the area known as the Outer World segment. It relates to the social world 'out there', the media, objective and practical knowledge, the world of finance and future planning. If someone has a large area here, so their palm is wedge shaped, they're likely to be highly sociable, talkative, rational, good with the media and with people, and full of nervous energy.

Sometimes the side of the palm opposite the thumb (known as the radial edge) bulges in the middle to give a curved shape. The best way to think of this formation is as a 'karate chop' palm. This exaggerates the outer axis of activity, where the two quadrants meet. This gives something of a 'steamroller' personality, someone who bulldozes over the opposition and who doesn't take 'no' for an answer. These people don't listen, they can be domineering and competitive and they have little time for the smaller issues in life.

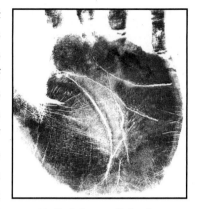

12. **Bulging radial edge**

On the other side of the palm below the index digit is the Ivory Tower zone.

This is about aspirations, personal power and influence. If this is enlarged, it indicates a personality concerned with their own way of doing things. They can be a bit of a control freak with a high opinion of themselves. Only the best is good enough in anything they posses and aspire to.

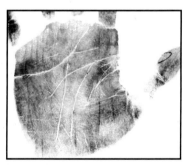

13. **Enlarged ivory tower zone**

OK, so what if you didn't find anything over-developed in the palm's form and the fingers were just sort of average, neither long nor short? Well don't worry, that's common and perfectly normal, you just continue on to the next level, the skin texture.

CHAPTER THREE

Taking the rough with the smooth...

The skin ridges

Skin quality is enormously important in palmistry. It indicates how finely tuned the central nervous system is and shows what sort of environment a person likes to be surrounded by. The skin on the surface of the palm is made up of a series of papillary ridges that contain various types of nerve sensor cells. The finer the grain of the skin's surface, the more acute and receptive the central nervous system of a person. The harder, coarser, and more wider spaced the skin ridges, the harder and coarser the world a person lives in and habitually comes into contact with. Of course, manual labour will cause the skin to develop calluses. However, the natural skin ridge density won't change.

Always check the skin by stroking the index finger of your right hand (the most sensitive fingertip) over an area in the centre of the palm where there are no calluses.

The skin is on a sliding scale of fineness, but palmists categorise it with four simple metaphors to make life easier. At the most sensitive end of the scale where you can't feel the skin ridges at all we have 'silk' skin which is thin, soft, delicate and extremely fine. Slightly less sensitive is 'paper' skin, which feels dry, smooth and papery - the skin ridges are barely detectable. Next comes 'grainy' skin, where you can feel the skin ridges easily, the palm is warm and dry and the lines well-marked. The most rough skin is 'coarse' skin; here the skin is very rough to the touch, the lines are deeply etched and only a few in number.

Silk

Silk skin creates a sensitive constitution, highly receptive to atmospheres. It's more common on women's palms then men's. Intuitive and aware, silk-skinned folk are somewhat delicate, they avoid conflict and harsh environments as much as possible. They appreciate finesse and luxury, and have a delicate palate. Such skin likes to caress, infer, respond and feel.

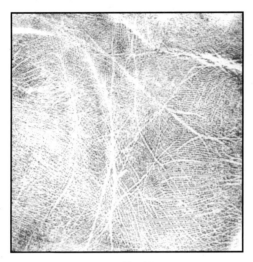

14. Silk skin

Paper

Skin that's fine, dry and often slightly yellowish where you can just perceive the skin ridges is paper skin.

This skin quality is common. It creates a responsiveness to visual and verbal stimuli. This type of palm touches paper, books, PC's, phones and connects to others

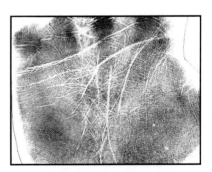

15. Paper skin

through the mass of media networks, however they can be a little distant and sometimes are wary of physical touch.

Grainy

Grainy skin is next. This skin ridges are clearly visible and easily felt. This type of palm is made to do, act, initiate and endeavour. Such skin is always found on busy people. This is someone responsive, who's always active and not particularly inward-looking or reflective. They're often very sporty and business-minded.

16. Grainy skin

Coarse

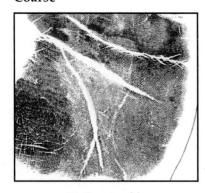

17. Coarse skin

Coarse skin touches brick, steel, wood and the raw earth. This skin type is rough and abrasive in nature and found almost exclusively on men. These people need to be outdoors and to be physically active. They are incredibly hardy and resilient, but not at all subtle, talkative, aware of others' feelings or very expressive. They often possess manual skills, have a good rapport with nature and animals and tend to prefer action to words.

CHAPTER FOUR

All fingers and thumbs...

The fingers

This is an area where vast advances have been made in understanding a person's psychology from their finger development.

The main qualities that need to be checked when examining the digits and thumbs are their length in relationship to each other and their stiffness.

The Thumb

Let's start with the thumb. The thumb stands in opposition to the fingers to form a gripping motion. Thumbs (in terms of their size and stiffness) indicate the extent of a person's 'grip' on themselves, their self-control and drive. The longer the thumb, the greater the capacity to dominate one's weaker impulses, personal circumstances and other people. The stiffness of the thumb shows how you apply your will - loosely in terms of a floppy thumb, or rigidly in terms of a stiff one.

The average length of the thumb is for it to reach anywhere between a third to half-way up the first phalange of the first finger when it's lain alongside it. If the thumb's long, it'll come close to the first joint of the index digit. If it's short, it'll only reach the base.

Highly motivated people have long thumbs, they don't need to be pushed. Short thumbs are rare, but will always show limited will and resolve. It's best these folk get them-selves 'under the thumb' of a longer-thumbed soul through positive group activity to achieve their aims.

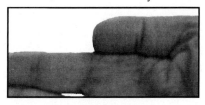

18. Short thumb

Flexibility

Stiffness is checked by simply pulling the thumb back toward the wrist. Most thumbs move back a few centimetres or so. When the thumb bends back almost to the wrist, it's a flexible thumb. When it won't bend back at all, it's a stiff thumb.

Floppy thumbed folk are easy going, laid-back people who don't like to exert themselves overmuch. They're found on those that work at doing things they enjoy. They're particularly common in the arts and on those that work in sociable, leisure and pleasure vocations as they're flexible and adaptable. However, they lack the will to go all-out to attain high achievements.

Stiff-thumbed people are stiff in their resolve. They tend to stick to a course of action once it's decided. They're persistent and push themselves hard, working to achieve personal goals without bending over backward for anyone else. They can always be relied upon to get the job done.

Checking the digits

When you find a finger shorter or longer than average, it's enormously significant. It indicates the particular way a person has evolved psychologically and shows adoptions in their attitudes to self (index), society (middle finger), status (ring) and speech (little finger). The fingers are highly revealing about childhood and formative influences.

In palmistry we used the metaphors of the MIRROR of self-consciousness, pride and power issues (index finger), the WALL of mental boundaries, norms and value systems (middle finger), the PEACOCK of persona, self-expression and attention-getting (ring finger) and the ANTENNA of sexual, signal and verbal communication (little finger).

In order to work out which digits are unusually long or short, you need to know the standard, average relative finger lengths. Normally, the index and ring fingers are almost the same length, with the ring finger just slightly longer (no more than half a centimetre) than the index. If the index looks the same length as the ring digit, or is just the slightest fraction longer, it's considered long.

The middle digit normally has half the top phalange jutting above a line drawn across the top of the ring and index digits. The little finger normally comes up to the second crease line of the ring finger.

You can easily check index and ring finger length by running a straight edge across the tip of these two digits, pushing the middle finger back out of the way. If the rule is level, the fingers are the same length and the index must be considered long. If it drops in either direction you can easily see which is the longer. Remember if the index is only a little shorter (up to half a centimetre) this is normal and average.

Draw a line along the straight edge where it crosses the middle finger, then you can see if the middle finger is long or short. You can also check the middle finger by looking at the back of the hand. The base of the fingernail on the middle finger should be just a millimetre or two below a line drawn across the tip of the ring and index fingers.

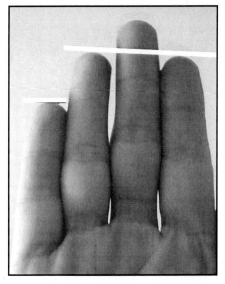

The little finger is easily checked by seeing if it reaches to the top crease of the neighbouring digit, but it can be complicated if it's unusually low set, deep into the palm. This will be explained in the section on the little finger.

19. Palm with all the fingers of average length

Mirror finger

This is the most important digit. It shows how you reflect yourself inwardly. It indicates the sort of mothering influence you've had. It rules pride, ambition, self-esteem and personal vision, the need to exert one's own values and qualities on the world around you. Control, self importance and personal responsibility are also bound up with this finger.

If the finger is long (even by only a tiny fraction than the peacock digit) there's a strong sense of needing to control situations and other people. Those with this finger long are intensely self-aware, self-conscious and self-obsessed with a natural sense of authority. They spend a lot of time in self-reflection and tend to be self-critical perfectionists.

Brain and digit development are scientifically linked to early development and the relationship with the primary mother figure.

When the mirror digit's long, childhood was marked by precocious over-awareness of self and sense of responsibility. Invariably the mother was exceptionally strong or there was an absent, ineffective mother figure. Either way, the individual developed an early responsible role and self-reliance. The long 'mirror' magnifies one's own flaws. Hence there can be a perennial sense of striving to get the respect and ideals required. It has been proven that long mirror-fingered people have higher than average levels of observation, tending to notice details of their surroundings to a greater extent than those without this feature. People with long mirror digits take themselves seriously and hate to be mocked. They don't trust superficial values like fame or popularity. They refuse to dress for effect, naturally mistrust the flashy and ostentatious and strive for responsible positions where personal standards can be applied.

Where the mirror finger is more than a half-centimetre shorter than the peacock finger, a person has a diminished sense of self-importance and deep-held feelings of inadequacy. The shorter the mirror finger, the more this is the case and the more they tend to feel they are the victim, rather than the motivator of their lives. There's an aversion to self-reflection, a marked lack of responsibility and poor attention to detail. It's an indicator of a childhood where one had little personal reinforcement of responsibility, little sense of personal power and an inadequate sense of individuality. This is where the primary parent was distracted by work, other siblings or other issues, where no one imbued a sense of authority, self importance or genuine responsibility, power and trust. The short finger can also show a 'spoiled' child, given too much without effort, ambition and integrity.

All aspects of self-neglect have been linked to the short mirror digit, including obesity, alcohol and drug dependency, depression and self-harm issues. One benefit of the finger being short, however, is that one never takes oneself too seriously and one can never be accused of being 'precious'. A short finger can be compensated for by constant reinforcement of self worth and consequently a host of aspiration lines will be seen running up off the earth line (these will be discussed later).

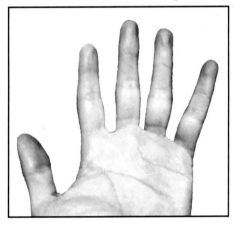

20. Short mirror digit (also long peacock and antenna digits)

Wall Digit

This is the longest digit; it rules normality, stability, values and balance. It's the digit least likely to be longer or shorter than average.

The wall finger represents the boundaries, barriers and mental constructs that give us a sense of normality. Lifestyle, work, convention, rules, authority, cultural and religious values are all bound up with this finger.

When the digit's long, there's a serious attitude to one's profession. This is found on those whose work involves intricate and detailed knowledge with lots of qualifications and certificates. The law, medicine, academia, science, research and administration and people who work within a hierarchy, bureaucracy or system all have a long wall digit.

When short, the mental attitude is anti rules and restrictions, they're much more likely to rebel or drop out of society. People with short 'wall' fingers often live away from their country of birth and are unconventional. They hate a life which is rule-bound and are often anarchists, socialists or other 'ists'. The short wall is also common on inventive, creative and anarchic individuals because they find innovative ways of doing things and approach life from a different angle.

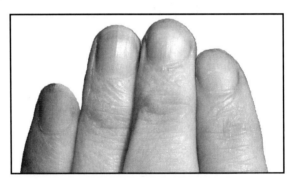

21. Short wall digit

Peacock digit
This digit is the measure of the persona, the public face of a person. Psychologically it's the display instinct in the competition to attract a mate.

It's related to all aspects of the drive to show off – developing skills, arts, aesthetics, creative expression, sporting prowess, risk taking and the sense of fun.

When long, there's a strong need for self-expression, but this like all aspects must be balanced against the rest of the palm (the palm in *Illustration 20* has a long peacock digit). Obviously, if someone has silk skin, they're not going to be a rock singer strutting their stuff on stage, but they may have a strong inclination to paint watercolours, for instance.

The media is massed with those with ring fingers of exaggerated length, as are all showbiz personalities, sales people, artists, actors, 'characters', and life and soul of the party people. Whenever you see anyone dressed outrageously, check their peacock digit, inevitably it's long. Long ring-fingered folk take risks in life as they don't value themselves as their index digit is relatively short.

Long peacock fingers need to be liked and to be popular. Long mirror fingers need to be taken seriously and to be respected. This is the profound difference between the two.

Antenna finger

This digit is concerned with communication, intimacy, sexuality and commerce - all of which are forms of dialogue. On a third of women and a tenth of men, the finger's low-set. It may look short at first glance, but could be of average length or even longer than average once you take the low setting into account. Check the setting by observing the first phalange crease (nearest the palm) of the little finger – it should be level with a point half-way up the base phalange of the ring digit.

Low-set antennas indicate something went wrong with the father-parent relationship. Either the father was emotionally absent or there was a deeply conditional, over-close relationship. A low-set digit shows a child-like immaturity in relationships, in intimacy and in articulating and understanding ones deepest needs. Often the use of language and articulacy develops twenty years late. Very often low-set little digit people enter relationships with older partners and find it difficult to express and understand their sexual and intimate selves. This can lead to unsatisfactory relationships until this process is analysed and understood.

When this digit's long, like a long antenna, it acquires and manipulates language skilfully (the palm in *Illustration 20* shows a long antenna digit). The length gives a love of words, eloquence, wit, sexual sophistication and financial acumen. A long finger here will often be involved in manipulating words, be it commerce, education, sales, writing or foreign language to great effect.

Where this finger's short, there's a poor appreciation of the subtleties of language. Communication can be limited and child-like. Often those with short antenna digits are uncertain with their finances. They tend avoid long words, sarcasm and irony. Verbal wit is usually in the form of memorised jokes.

Finger flexibility
The flexibility of the fingers demonstrates mental flexibility. Fingers which hardly move back when you push against them show high, long-term stress levels; rigid mental processes and a lack of spontaneity. Rigid fingers make for a rigid, bloody-mindedness.

Where the fingers are floppy and bend back 45 degrees or more, it shows an impulsive mind. Open, spontaneous and free, this is a person delightfully receptive to new ideas but psychologically all over the place, never sticking to any view, structure or opinion.

Bent fingers
A sideways bend (assuming it's not the result of arthritis or accident) bends mental attitudes in a particular direction. The most common bend is the mirror finger bending toward the wall digit - this indicates the sense of self (mirror) is dependent on society (wall) for approval. It shows lack of confidence and a

need for support. There's reluctance to stand alone, fearfulness of fulfilling one's own potential and often a materialistic acquisitiveness.

When the middle digit bends toward the ring finger there are always clashes with authority and problems settling into the right job and life path. Such folk often try to follow a conventional route, but feel let down by society and lack faith in authority.

When the peacock digit bends toward the wall digit the sense of fun, pleasure and self-expression is put aside for the demands of duty, work and family. It can create a martyr complex.

Sometimes the antenna finger bends toward the peacock. This gives the capacity to bend the truth for effect. It can make for an outright liar but also a diplomatic charmer, always able to say the right thing at the right time.

CHAPTER FIVE

Whorls, arches and loops...

Brain waves

The print patterns on the palm and fingers are crucial in modern palmistry. Scientific research links particular patterns with particular psychological attitudes and medical conditions. The print patterns are called dermatoglyphics (from the Greek: derma-skin, glyph-markings) and are best visualised as brain-wave formations. The shape of the print patterns shows the nature and shape of a person's conceptual process.

First, let's take a look at the different types of print patterns. Every print on every palm in the world is unique, so any print you look at will differ very slightly from the examples illustrated here. However, all prints can be categorised into one of five basic formations.

22. Simple arch

23. Loop

24. Whorl

25. Double loop composite

26. Tented arch

Tented arches and simple arches look alike on first glance, but tented arches are steeply inclined, where simple arches have a much flatter incline. Loops are split into radial and ulna loops. Radial loops are exactly the same as ulna loops but they face in the opposite direction. The open end of the loop faces the thumb on a radial loop. Radial loops are rarer than ulna loops.

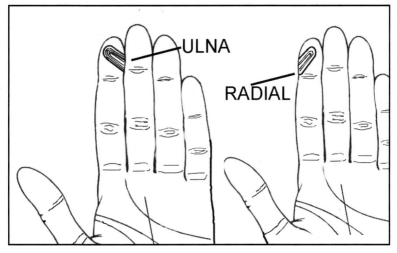

27. Radial loop, ulna loop

Now let's look at the psychological attitude each print pattern creates. The effect of each pattern varies according to where it's placed.

Tented Arches
These form a sharp spike pointing skyward - 'spiky', reactive, the impulse to shock, surprise and impress, the need to break out of boundaries, to be prominent, to be noticed, enthusiastic, fanatical, excitable, intense, restless, extreme.

Composite
Formed by two loops facing in opposite directions - cycles of enthusiasm and disappointment, moodiness, mentally never

certain of anything, difficulty in making decisions, a wise, anti-fanatic, universal viewpoint.

Ulna Loop
A wave shape - empathic, gregarious, relationships with others prioritized, adaptable, receptive and impressionable, a need to belong.

Radial Loop
A wave moving in the opposite direction to normal - hyper-receptive to others, unduly sensitive to criticism, insecure, unstable, caring, giving, over-performing for others, hyper responsive.

Whorl
A series of ever-decreasing circles or a spiral formation. A variation on the whorl is known as a peacock's eye. It's still a whorl, but its circles are trapped within a loop - self involved, isolated, needs space and freedom, original, disconnected, different, individual, talented, secretive, self motivated, self-centred.

Simple Arch
A flat, chevron shape - deep, fixed, materialistic, stubborn, loyal, emotionally repressed, faithful, persistent, practical, unassuming.

Most fingers and thumbs have an ulna loop on them. Simply ignore these as they're so common as to be normal and average. Every other pattern is significant though, and has a major influence on character. Remember each print only affects the part of the palm (and related area of the mind) it's found on. The most important prints are on the mirror fingers and thumbs, because they affect how a person thinks of themselves (mirror) and how they put plans into effect (thumb).

Now let's look at the meaning of the most common variations of print patterns you're likely to find.

Mirror finger's print pattern
Whorl
Marked sense of individuality, secretive, single-minded, a need for space. Difficulty in taking orders, happy with own company, prefer to work alone or unsupervised.

Simple arch
Cautious, stubborn, unpretentious, self-effacing, reliable, loyal, family orientated. A skilled pair of hands. Emotionally blocked, somewhat old-fashioned.

Radial loop
Hyper-receptive to others, insecure, identifies with other's needs. A 'people person', super-nice, a carer, though can be touchy, finds criticism unbearable; can't say 'no'.

Composite
Uncertain about who one is, philosophical, unable to make one's own life decisions, a marked impartiality and diplomacy.

Tented arch
Intense, takes things too far, excessive, over the top, fascinated by any form of personal transformation, likes to entertain, teach, or motivate others, charismatic, needs excitement.

The thumb's print pattern
Whorl
Acts independently, self motivated, needs to demonstrate independence, innovative and original in approaching new projects.

Simple arch
Extremely stubborn, thorough, persistent, practical in approaching tasks, not afraid to get hands dirty.

Composite
A two-way mind-set, inconsistent, easily persuaded out of a course of action, a vacillating attitude. Difficult to be 100% committed to anything or anyone.

The wall finger's print pattern
Whorl
Disregards dogma, rules and convention, odd or unusual beliefs and lifestyles. Freedom always more important than worldly success. Follows a non-traditional spiritual path.

Simple arch
Straightforward, simple, and pragmatic attitude to work and lifestyle. A serious, secure, well paid job is important. Has a sense of duty and likes order, method and fairness in values. Justice and fairness important. Wants a stable lifestyle.

Radial loop
Culture, lifestyle, and values never secure and entirely open. Easily adapts to different lifestyles, careers and other cultures. Usually over-conformist or strongly alternative.

Composite
Has a perennial sense of questioning and doubt about career, philosophy, values and lifestyle.

The peacock finger's print pattern
Whorl
Individual and original in creativity, dress, music and the arts. Has good spatial awareness and a flair for design and imagery.

Simple arch

Has a need for physical expression. Likely to love archaic skills and admires traditional art forms and old fashioned iconography. A love of historic and classical ideals of beauty.

The antenna finger's print pattern
Whorl

Enjoys 'insider' knowledge and specialised language. Reticent sexually but intensely curious. Endures long periods without intimacy, interspersed with frantically passionate episodes. Drawn to unconventional relationships.

CHAPTER SIX

Patterns on the palm...

Prints on the palm

Everyone has prints on their fingertips, but very often there are prints on the palm as well. When you read palm prints you relate each pattern to the zone of the palm it's situated on. Most of them are on the Sea of Subconscious area, but they can be found on the other zones as well.

Interdigital loops

These are very common and are little loops that fall at the point where the fingers are joined by a web of skin.

Loop of leisure

This is a loop situated between the peacock and wall digits. It heightens the pleasure principle and makes one prioritise leisure time. Hobbies, crafts, skills and sports are important. Often the leisure pursuit eventually becomes a profession. With this sign, enjoyment comes before career prospects.

Loop of industry

Situated between the wall and peacock digits this is the mark of someone that takes their work seriously. Career and industriousness are a kind of pleasure. Usually career choice is a serious, industrious one.

Loop of leadership

A much rarer marking that the two previous ones. This loop is found between the mirror and wall digits. It shows a natural organisational ability and the knack of acquiring status or respect within a group.

**28. Loop of leadership,
between mirror and wall
digits**

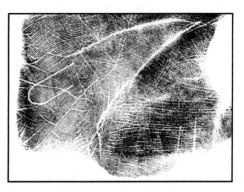

29. Loop of sensitivity

Loop of sensitivity

A loop found around half way up the palm below the peacock or antenna digit. It indicates a heightened awareness, also a sense of déjà vu. Psychic perception is possible as is artistic responsiveness.

Whorl of isolation

This is a whorl in the middle of the Sea of Subconscious area. This is a signal of a soul fascinated by dreams, the deeper realms of the mind, spirituality and the subconscious. It's hard to develop intimacy with anyone that has this marking, there's a

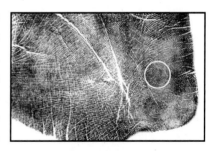

30. Whorl of isolation

need to be deeply private. It's a strongly creative marking, more often than not found on writers and actors. Often those with this sign get trapped inside themselves, or trapped in shallow ostentation outside their deeper natures.

Loop of nature

This loop faces outward and is found on the very outer edge of the palm. It's a sign of receptivity to the earth's energies, and a love of nature. Always there's a gift for dowsing and healing, also a feel for energy points in the body and in the Earth. Usually there's a fascination with mystery and the unknown.

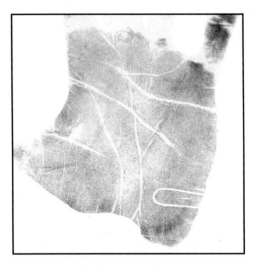

31. Loop of nature

Composite on Sea of Subconscious

This is rare. It gives constant emotional ups and downs and confusion about deeper feelings. There's always difficulty in maintaining a stable emotional bond and often consequent unstable relationships. The composite gives openness to both genders emotionally and often one is fascinated by gender, sexuality and psychology.

Arch on Sea of Subconscious

The repressive arch makes for a somewhat closed personality, never opening up about deeper needs and drives. There's a need to express energy physically. It's common on midwives, masseurs and carers.

Loop of inspiration

Like a fountain of inspiring impressions, this loop rises up from the bottom of the palm. It's common on artists and musicians, spiritual seekers and those fascinated by and open to mystical experiences.

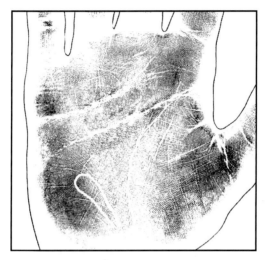

32. Loop of inspiration

Loop of rhythm

This is found on the bottom edge of the primal Home, Body and Family quadrant. It shows a strong sense of rhythm and a love of music.

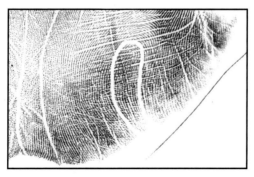

33. Loop of rhythm

Loop of battle

A loop in the web of skin just above and near to the thumb is a marker of drive and energy – someone who is physically courageous, who seeks and needs challenges.

When you've identified the print patterns on both palms, compare the two and look for differences. Like all aspects of the palms that change from the passive to the active, these differences explain the contradictions between the inner and outer personalities.

CHAPTER SEVEN

Lines of life and lines of love...

The Lines

Now we'll move onto the lines of the palm. First of all though, some general points.

The lines aren't static, they change and develop throughout one's lifetime.

There are four major lines and many minor lines. If a major line is weak or missing, a person will struggle in life until that line forms. The lack of a minor line though, is of no consequence.

Any line that runs all the way across the palm from side to side or top to bottom creates an obsessive, intense, driven personality.

The quality of a line highlights the quality of the person's experience. For instance, if someone has a weak, poor quality, islanded Line of Emotion, they experience a weak, muddled and moody emotional life.

Got that? OK. Now we'll look at two common hand patterns, full palms and empty palms.

Full palms

A full palm is one covered in a web of fine lines all over its surface. It indicates a highly strung, complex, sensitive, easily-overloaded person-ality. Full hands are found on those that are mentally overactive, they're usually not very physical people.

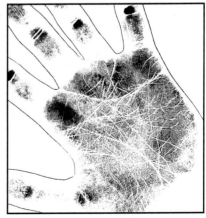

34. Full palm

Empty hands

Empty palms are generally (but not always) found on manual workers. They're straightforward folk, lacking psychological complexity. They tend to be habitual, and like to see the world in simple, physical terms, and through simple absolute philosophies, avoiding self-analysis and too much introspection. Illustration 17 is an empty palm.

Race and Gender

It's normal for those of African, Asian and South American descent to possess simple hands. As this is normal it wouldn't be commented on in a reading. Generally, women have more full hands than men and the passive palm practically always has more lines on it than the active hand.

Roots and shoots – the Vitality Line.

This line, traditionally called the Lifeline, shows by its length and strength a person's development of stability, security and basic physical vitality. When the line's short and weak, it's hard to create a stable lifestyle. Good health, a stable family and a secure home are longed for, but elusive. They tend to be 'all over the place' with bouts of exhaustion and a sense that nothing lasts. Those with short, weak Vitality Lines live highly mobile, changeable, often exciting lifestyles, quick to seize opportunities and ready to snatch at dreams and make new starts.

The line starts at the skin between the thumb and index digit and runs in a semicircle around the thumb ball. It should be imagined as a root, channelling the energy stored in the mount.

If there isn't much of a Vitality Line, there's little stamina and always deep-held insecurity. A short line indicates a rootless person. A weak, short Vitality Line on the passive hand is a sure sign of an unstable, insecure childhood without enough parental guidance, re-assurance or stability. Ungrounded, unrealistic and lacking common sense, 'cosmic' types, highly alternative folk, and perennial travellers tend to have short, weak earth lines.

Establishing fixed physical routines of exercise, diet and sleep strengthens a Vitality Line in a matter of months.

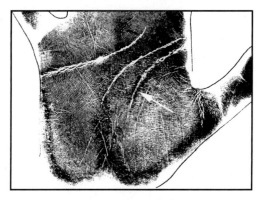

35. A poor quality Vitality Line

If the Vitality Line's long and strong, a person is a well-rooted soul with feet firmly on the ground, an instinct for homemaking and the energy to make a good, stable life for themselves.

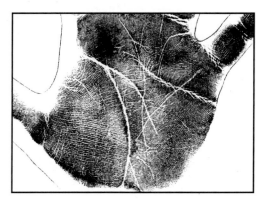

36. A good quality Vitality Line

If there's a fork (as in Illustration 36) moving outward from the base of the line, it shows a travel orientated, restless, but adventurous spirit. It's as if the root is reaching out for new territory. The opposite case, where the bottom of the line has no branches, and is very deep, thick and red shows a 'stick-in-the-mud' who hates leaving home.

Sometimes (again in *Illustration 36*) the Vitality Line sweeps much wider around the thumb ball than normal. It's a sign of abundant warmth and lust for life, as if the line's bursting with energy.

The Vitality Line is the only line on the palm that can be marked chronologically with any degree of accuracy. The beginning at the top is year zero and the base where the line ends is around age 84.

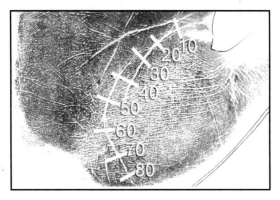

37. Timing on the Vitality Line

Breaks (as in *Illustration 37*) in the Vitality Line aren't always bad news. They signal interruptions in the course of our lives, but if the line overlaps and becomes stronger after the break, the disruption leads to a more abundant, vital lifestyle.

The main reasons for breaks on the Vitality Line are serious life changes that interrupt our rhythm: loss of a parent or sibling, divorce, illness, moving house or change in family circumstance.

Don't make predictions based on markings on the Vitality Line. We create our own fate. Healthy patterns of diet, sleep and exercise will improve the Vitality Line, often repairing breaks and weak areas.

The Line of Emotion

The Line of Emotion (often known as the Heart Line) shows whether someone's a giver or a taker, sincere, faint-hearted or romantic. Like all markings, it must be read in reference to other palm points, especially the skin texture. A horny-handed man-of-the-outdoors with coarse skin will never intuit your hidden hurts, hovering gently with caresses and whispered poetry, however clear, strong and well-marked his Line of Emotion.

This line is about how we process our feelings. It's metaphor is a river that floods us with impressions of the exterior world, indicating how we respond emotively to a crying child, a moving aria or the scent of lavender. The line's length, depth and strength show the amount and intensity of the emotional response. Obviously, someone with a long, deep, red line will feel more strongly than someone with a weak, short line.

If the Line of Emotion is deeper and stronger than the other lines on the palm, it shows someone dominated by their feelings. They're passionate, responsive and warm-hearted, but everything would depend on mood. Irrational behaviour is likely, energy would wax and wane with the emotions. People with dominant lines of emotion put enormous emphasis on the quality, depth and resonance of their experience. People with dominant lines of consciousness put the emphasis on the logic, practicality and fiscal cost of their experiences.

The line starts under the antenna digit, but varies greatly in where it ends. A long line would end somewhere under

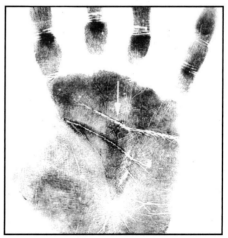

38. A dominant Line of Emotion

the mirror digit, signalling a person with a large range of emotional responses, a lot of friends and one who deeply involves themselves in the social world. If the line crosses the palm completely from side to side, it shows a compulsion to give and respond to others. This is often found on carers and therapists.

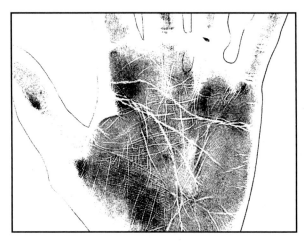

39. A long Line of Emotion

A short line one would end somewhere under the wall digit and indicates a person who is connected to a small circle of people, usually only family, relatives and neighbours.

Very short lines are found on socially-isolated souls.

Short lines of emotion (like the lower section of the line in *Illustration 40*) are less enduring than long, deep ones – they might be your best friend one moment and forget that you exist the next! A long line holds on to relationships for a long time.

The more messy and complicated the Line of Emotion, with breaks, islands and crossing lines, the more complicated a person is emotionally. A broken-up line means a person's much more likely to wander in their affections and be emotionally unstable. Often poor quality lines of emotion denote the tendency to drink excessively.

If the Line of Emotion has a break in it, there's a break in an individual's ability to feel for a period of time. There's been a loss or disappointment emotionally, like divorce or death of a close one

Lines which curve upwards are expressive, demonstrative, and somewhat 'Italian' emotively. They are clear about their gender role and highly focused emotionally. Probably the ideal point for the line to end is between the mirror and wall fingers.

Straight (as in *Illustration 38*) or dropping lines of emotion tend to express emotions through action, doing favours, or buying gifts. They're more reticent about directly expressing their feelings, and tend to be more sexually androgynous. They like emotional signals that are clear and direct. They find it hard to focus exclusively on the 'right one', spreading their affections widely.

Sometimes there are two parts to the Line of Emotion - a lower and higher section. It shows someone operating on two emotional levels. They have a more superficial side (the higher part of the line) where they're socially active and, apparently expressive, but there's a deeper, more reticent and complex level of feeling that's rarely shown.

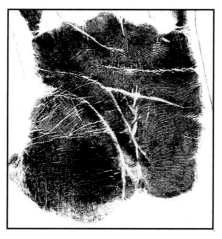

40. A doubled Line of Emotion

Jealousy on the palm is easily seen by a branch or ending of the line running down towards or onto the Vitality Line. These show emotionally insecurity and the expectation or experience of severe emotional loss. People with this marking can't let go.

If the Line of Emotion runs up into the mirror digit, it shows high emotional expectations. Such souls put the object of their affections on a pedestal but can, alas, be sadly disappointed.

If the line curves up into the wall finger, there's an emphasis on practicality in the emotions. This isn't an emotionally adventurous spirit, but one often inclined to marry a distant relative, school-friend or neighbour.

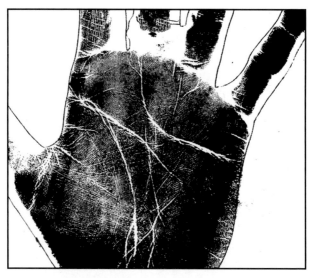

41. A Line of Emotion ending at the wall digit

A sign to watch out for is a ray of small lines near the end of the line. This indicates a tremendous flirt, someone that needs to connect to lots of potential partners.

The Line of Emotion is rarely singular and without islands, breaks or multiple endings. This reflects the difficult, mechanised and money-orientated world we live in, so unsuited to the life of the heart.

CHAPTER EIGHT

Light beams and life-paths...

The Line of Consciousness

The Line of Consciousness (traditionally called the Head Line) is the most important line on the palm. It shows the way we think and this is of course a major aspect of our personality.

The metaphor to use for this line is a light beam. The clarity depth, extent and direction of our mental vision is shown by this line.

It starts at the edge of the palm just above or connected to the top of the Vitality Line. It's long when it crosses the palm to end somewhere under the antenna digit. A short line will end under the wall digit. Someone with a long line thinks a lot and projects their ideas a long way ahead, taking many factors into account. There's lots of mental processing going on. Long, clear lines of consciousness are found on pensive, philosophical types, writers, consultants and questioners of the status quo, they speculate endlessly. Long lines deal in abstract thought and look into the future.

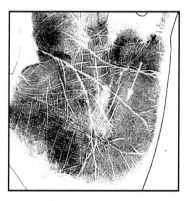

42. A long Line of Consciousness

Any islands, breaks or fuzzy areas will destroy clarity of thought. However long this line, if it's of poor quality, a person can't focus or think clearly. The quality of this line shows an individual's ability to make money, get on in the world, express their own opinions, rationalise and assert themselves. A poor quality line indicates a person who functions less effectively and who lacks the confidence to express themselves fully – ideas tend to be borrowed; they are at the mercy of more focused personalities.

A short line shows a narrow area of mental focus. This is a mind that deals in the real, the concrete and the tangible. A short line doesn't speculate, philosophise or worry about the long-term implications. They *apply* ideas. Short, strong, clear lines of consciousness are found on doers: business people, skilled workers, technicians, and tradesmen – they tend to be highly effective people who expect a lot from life and work very hard. However, they don't see the bigger picture as their world view is limited.

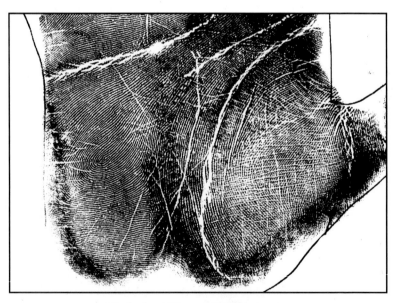

43. A short Line of Consciousness

On the level or round the bend?

Bent and straight lines of consciousness see the world differently. A straight line (as in *Illustration 42*) shows thinking to be level-headed, unemotional, to the point and rational. There's always an insistence on the facts. Their thinking is direct, following a chain of logic.

If the Line of Consciousness crosses the palm completely from one side to the other it signals an obsessive mentally. They can have a blind insistence on their way of seeing things and find it hard to see other's viewpoints. They cut off themselves from their deeper feelings and simply can't stop thinking. An apparent calm obscures deep held tensions.

People with bent lines of consciousness see the world bent through the filter of their own experiences, perceptions and memories. They love the artistic and the mystical; they enjoy ambiguity, poetry, metaphor and moody lighting. They 'navel gaze' and delve deeply into their inner reflections. Bent lines make mental connections that are intuitive and imaginative. The

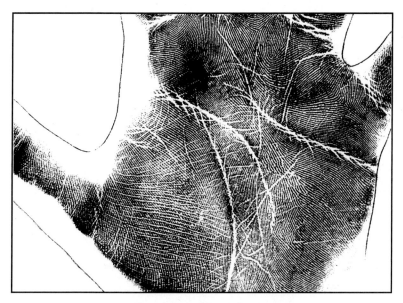

44. Bent Line of Consciousness

more the line is bent, the more the personal, private and deep realms colour the consciousness. Artists, poets, psychoanalysts, very private people, those that spend a lot of time alone, and those fascinated by their inner lives tend to have bent lines of consciousness.

Occasionally the line is doubled or forked. This shows someone with mental versatility and an ability to hold multiple viewpoints. This is a mind that can operate on more than one level, often to the extent there seems to be two personalities.

Beginnings

The gap between the beginning of the Line of Consciousness and the Vitality Line demonstrates the extent of psychological adventurousness. The greater the gap, the more aspirational, adventurous and independent the person. A large gap of a centimetre or more (as in *Illustration 43*) is a mark of a person's confidence in their own opinions and shows how they've moved away in every sense from their roots to form their own, self-created set of values, friends and lifestyle.

The more the Line of Consciousness sticks to the Vitality Line (like the one in *Illustration 42*), the more a person mentally stays in the realm they know. Clinging lines show extreme caution, little confidence in one's own opinions and someone easily talked out of their decisions. It's often the sign of dominating parents.

A break in the line shows a difficult time where one can't think and function, usually through some serious breakdown. When the Line of Consciousness changes direction abruptly or changes its form, the personality undergoes a similar change.

Islands on the line are always a sign of stress, as if the mind is 'blowing things up' out of proportion.

Rarely, in around one person in a hundred, you'll see the Line of Consciousness and the Line of Emotion fuse into a single line. This is known as a simian line. It's the sign of a deeply repressive and obsessive personality. Thought and feeling are fused together so they carry everything to extremes. Simian-lined folk are exceptional in the strength, single-mindedness and focus they bring to whatever they do, to the exception of everything else. They put their whole heart and mind into any project. It's often the sign of a great achiever, but it's difficult for them to accept change and even more difficult for them to be objective. People with simian lines should always be encouraged to relax as there are great inner tensions at work.

The Life-path Line

This line (traditionally called the Fate Line or Saturn Line) is the most difficult major line to identify, as it's so varied and often poorly formed. It can start from somewhere in the middle of the palm, or from the Vitality Line, or from within the Sea of Subconscious area. It always moves vertically up the centre of the palm and points toward the wall finger, and this is how you'll recognise it. The Life-path Line shows how well you know

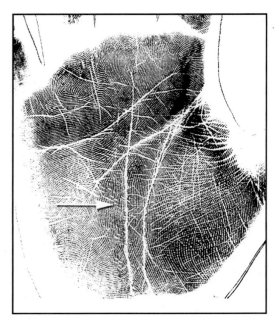

45. Long, straight centrally placed Life-path Line

yourself, how clearly your character is defined, and how much energy you put into your personal goals.

A long, strong, straight line from the base of the palm up through the middle shows someone who is a 'straight', clear, well defined character. They're hard working, reliable, trustworthy, honest, clear about themselves and very well-balanced. A straight line will avoid extreme behaviour and attitudes and will walk a straight path in life.

A weak, poorly-formed line shows someone who isn't clear who they are and who doesn't know what they want. It's impossible to be fulfilled if you don't have a clear Life-path Line.

Often when the line's particularly scratchy and weak, it shows someone in a prestigious career. However, they're burning themselves out, striving to attain the glittering heights of success. It's society's, the ad man's or the parent's idea of success though, and not their own, and this eventually leads to exhaustion.

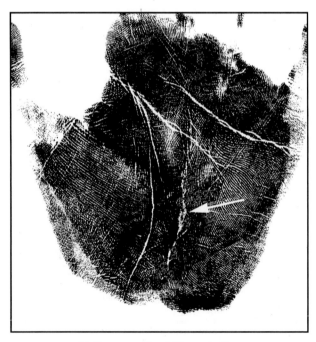

46. Poor quality Life-path Line

This line's associated with the career, as this is a major way of defining oneself. A clear Life-path Line doesn't necessarily mean a brilliant career, but a strong character with well-defined personal choices and the character to get what they personally want out of life.

If the line starts in the Sea of Subconscious, it marks a personality who prioritizes social connections, personal fulfilment and adaptability in life. It shows a job choice and lifestyle opposed to parental ideals. A line from this area gives a nature good with people and sociable with a large circle of friends. Anyone who works with the public, who uses social connections, who acquires work through a good reputation and who draws on their creativity has this marking. Usually a line from the Sea of Subconscious marks a work pattern that is distinctly non 9-5.

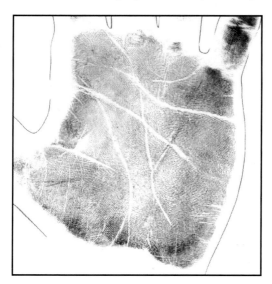

47. Life-path Line starting in Sea of Subconscious area

When the line begins joined to the Vitality Line, it indicates a life path based on parental expectation, security, the need to provide for family, and the drive for stability. This pathway often means spending a long time in training and in university getting qualifications. Usually the vocation is in large companies, corporations and public bodies. Life choices are based on practical needs and a sense of duty comes before everything.

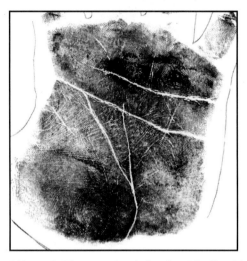

48. Life-path Line starting joined to Vitality Line

Frequently you'll find the Life-path Line appearing half way up the palm, with no indications below. This shows one discovering themselves mid-life, from then on knowing who they are and what they want.

Occasionally, you'll find a Life-path Line that's over-developed, so it's the strongest line on the palm. Alternatively the line travels all the way from the bottom of the palm to the base of the wall digit. This indicates an overly-fixed, inflexible character, one often fascinated by the idea of destiny. They tend to find it hard to adapt and plod though their lives with a kind of dull-minded steadfastness. It always gives unshakeable strength of character, but there's a need for more flexibility and opportunism in their life choices.

It's quite common to see a new line from the Sea of Subconscious area *joining* the Life-path Line at an angle. This indicates a change of direction in life. The change is always toward personal fulfilment and about letting go of burdens and received ideas. Also, life-changing new relationships are shown by this same marking.

Islands in the line indicate periods of unemployment, confusion and a lack of any sense of identity.

The Life-path Line is found in a good, clear formation on less and less people in the modern world. This is a consequence of the lack of time we have to get to know ourselves. Also it's due to the commercial, social and parental pressures that strangle the impulse to know who one really is.

Whenever you find the Life-path Line missing, advise a person to spend time in a different environment away from all current influences, in a situation where they can test themselves. In this way they can get to know what they're really made of.

CHAPTER NINE

Minor, but not unimportant...

The minor lines

We'll start with four essential points about the minor lines.

Any and all of the minor lines could be missing, this is normal.

The minor lines are faint, scratchy, easily missed and vary hugely in formation.

Minor lines change much more quickly than the major lines.

No minor line should be stronger than the major lines - it's a signal of a psychological or health issue that stops them functioning normally.

We'll start with the minor lines on the fingertips and work our way down to the base of the palm.

Fingertip Bars

Often you'll see small horizontal lines on the fingertips. These are a sign of the endocrinal system being overactive. At the menopause or at adolescence, this is normal. However, at any other time these marking are a sign of severe stress or exhaustion.

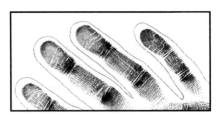

49. Fingertip Bars

Mid-phalange Activity Lines

These are fine, vertical lines on the middle finger phalanges (as in

Illustration 49). They're an indication of a very busy person, always planning ahead, and always on the go.

Samaritan Lines

These are very common. They're a series of fine, vertical lines crossing the Line of Emotion under the antenna digit. There needs to be three or four to make them worthy of comment. Samaritan lines are associated with carers of all kinds – therapists, nurses, healers, kindly people and simple 'good neighbours'.

50. Samaritan Lines

Ring of Solomon

This is a rare sign. It's a fine semi-circular line around the base of the mirror finger. It shows the ability to put oneself aside and develop insight into the nature of others. There's always a natural inclination to analyse, and an interest in psychology. It's common on

51 Ring of Solomon

counsellors, astrologers, palmists and the like.

Teacher's square

These aren't really true squares, but a formation of four inter-secting fine lines under the mirror finger. This marking signals the qualities of people management and is a good one to see in a manager or teacher.

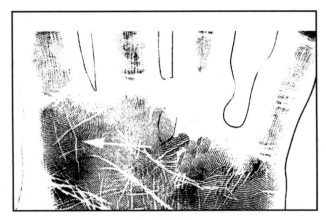

52. Teacher's Square

Mirage Line

These are found above and parallel to the Line of Emotion (as in *Illustration 52*). Often there are lots of faint lines, sometimes just one continuous single line. Mirage lines indicate a vivid imagi-nation, and a need to escape the mundane, physical world through, for instance, meditation and spirituality, drink or drugs, dreams, art or some other form of escapist activity. It gives a heightened sense of luxury and adds refinement. This line tends to be a signal of introversion. If the line's fragmented it shows someone highly strung, sensitive and sympathetic to others. Whenever this line's in a strong, bold formation a person is never quite fully present.

Affection Lines

Affection lines can be seen on the extreme outer edge of the palm, beneath the antenna finger. Almost everyone has one or two of these. However, only if the line extends three centimetres or more into the body of the palm is it worth examination.

A long straight line (over 3cm. long) makes for a seemingly endless search for the 'right' partner. This issue will dominate a person's relationships until the perfect partner is found, usually mid-life. From then on marital bliss will ensue with both partners utterly devoted.

If the line plunges down, ending close to or crossing the Line of Emotion, it gives a subliminal inclination toward a difficult martial relationship. There's a strong likelihood of divorce and only after this difficult experience can lasting love be found.

If the line curls up around the antenna digit it means one will find it difficult to attain intimacy with another. One is likely to remain outside the mating game for long periods; or one may find oneself in a celibate relationship.

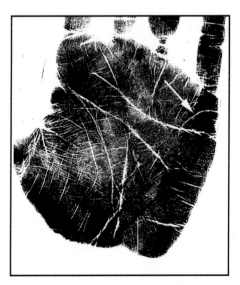

53. An Affection Line that plunges downward

Passion Line

This one always gets people going! It's an angular line running from mid way along the Line of Emotion moving up toward the antenna digit. It gives a highly visual, voyeuristic and imaginary aspect to a person's sexuality. Partners are chosen because of their physical attractiveness. It doesn't give a high sex drive necessarily, but there is always sexual curiosity.

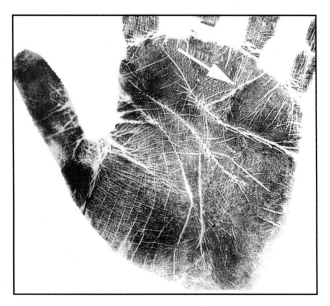

54. A good example of a Passion Line

Inner Realm Line

This line is a straight, fine, line running vertically up to the base of the peacock digit. It's nearly always present above the Line of Emotion, but only if the line extends down beneath that line is it noteworthy (there's a good example in *Illustration 51*). Its presence gives a sense of oneness, the ability to forget oneself, a need for peace and quiet, internal contentment, the need to be alone, an inner life. Meditators, artists, those that love their own company and those that have found a sense of peace develop this line.

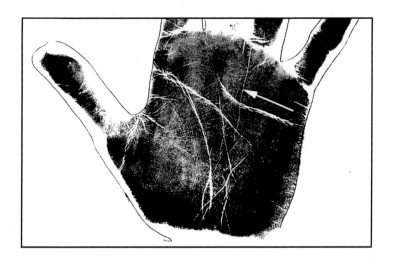

55. An Inner Realm Line

Nervous Activity Line

This line is present in many people's palms, and is almost always present in the elderly. It's a single line or a series of fine lines anywhere in the region from the base of the Vitality Line to the base of the little finger. It's hugely varied in form, often just a short line of a centimetre or two, or there may be a ladder like pattern of fine lines extending from palm base to antenna digit. If there's a single fine straight line (as in *Illustration 36*), it indicates the capacity for mental concentration and inspiration, a kind of lateral thinking. It's found in this form on mentally acute, inventive and inspired people. If (as in *Illustration 56* and is much more common) there is one trough-like line or lots of scratchy lines, it illustrates a

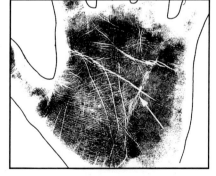

56. A poor quality Nervous Activity Line

nervous agitation that seriously affects the digestion and breathing process, excess stomach acid or not enough, possible asthma and poor liver function.

Spirit Line

This is easily confused with the previous line, but it's different in that it's a single clear, *semi circular* line originating in the Sea of Subconscious area and extending up toward the antenna digit. It shows psychic perception and intuitive potential. It's a very rare marking.

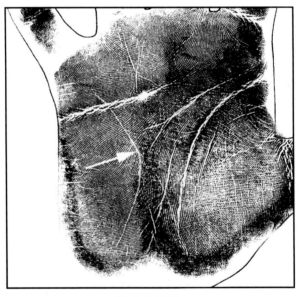

57. Spirit Line

Aspiration lines

These take the form of fine, hair-like lines rising up from the Vitality Line pointing towards the mirror finger. They are always positive in that they show new 'shoots' of budding enterprises to attain a new job, new child, a bigger house, better situation, positive attitudes and achievements.

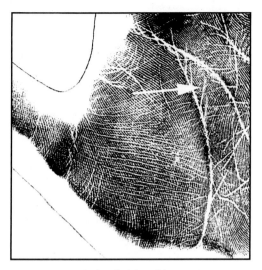

58. Aspiration Lines

Battle Line

This line is found within the upper half circle section of the Vitality Line, close to the thumb. Only if clear and unbroken and longer than two centimetres is it relevant. It's a sign of physical drive, a battling nature, the need for challenges; it's prevalent amongst athletes and sports people. If very strong or if there are lines connecting it to the Line of Consciousness, it can show excessive aggression and a defensive attitude.

59. Battle Line

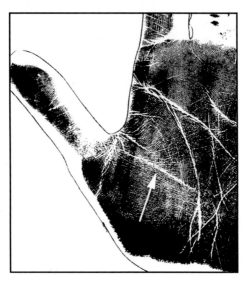

Loyalty Line

This is very common. It's a broad, horizontal line or crease crossing the Home, Body and Family quadrant, often touching the Vitality Line. It's a sign of an instinctive, tribal loyalty, which may be to the local football team, partner, family or home.

60. Loyalty Line

Domestic Stress Lines

Most people have a couple of fine lines running across the primal home and body quadrant. However, when you see a lot of these, it shows too much stress within the home environment and in general lifestyle.

Intensity Line

This line is quite common. It's a fine, horizontal, straight, line in the Sea of Subconscious. It shows stress in the emotional field, an inability to relax,

61. Stress Lines in the home and body quadrant

the need to be stimulated and stirred up. People with this line have a lot of get up and go, they seek excitement and love the hint of danger. Often you'll find this line in deep sea divers, aerobics instructors, racing drivers and skiers - anything to stimulate the senses.

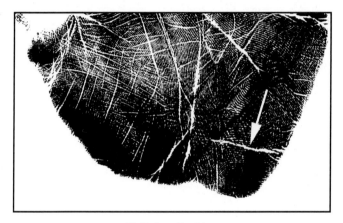

62. Intensity Line

Allergy Line

This line is found in the same place as the intensity line, but in this case it's a curved line. It's a sure sign of an over-responsive immune system and generally, the presence of allergies.

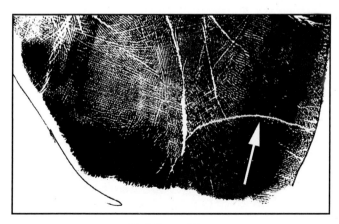

63. Allergy Line

Random markings

Most palms feature strange stars, circles, squiggles and unidentifiable markings - this is one of the aspects of the uniqueness of human beings. Don't be too concerned about these. You can make a guess at the meaning of a marking from its location on the palm. If it's on the primal Home, Body and Family area for instance, it can only relate to this area of a person's life. Bar lines, where a short line crosses a major line, show obstacles to be overcome. Crosses show two opposing directions and the need to make a decision. Dots show minor disasters caused by rage and very temporary loss of control. Islands are signs of confusion and stress. However, the major markings, the finger length, major lines, etc. are always much more important than random markings, so don't get lost in these.

CHAPTER TEN

All together now...

The incredible potency of palm reading begins when you put all the points together and build a picture.

When you look at someone's palm, work through the hand in the same order as you've learned each stage in this book - hand shape, skin texture, fingers, etc. That way you'll build a complete picture of the individual. Each level you uncover affects the next point you observe. If, for instance, you find a Line of Emotion that's stronger than all the other lines on the palm, this shows someone who's highly subjective and whose heart rules their head. However, if the skin texture is coarse and the thumb ball muscular, we're looking at the hands of, for example, a boat builder who senses the weather and who knows the moods of the sea. This person rarely expresses their sentiments verbally.

However, if the skin texture is silk, the thumb ball flat and the antenna digit long, we're probably looking at a poet who paints pictures with words in a highly elaborate and perceptive manner. The skin quality, print patterns and finger lengths all affect the interpretation of the lines and must be drawn into the picture you make of the personality.

Every point you observe about a palm affects the observations you make afterwards. If you read a palm methodically, you won't miss anything.

Always check the active against the passive hand and note any differences. Lines that are stronger, longer or clearer on the active than the passive show positive development, where somebody has worked and is working to overcome an area of weakness. If the Line of Emotion is very poor and short on the passive hand, but deep, long and strong on the active, they've spent a lot of time socialising with others and on being open to their feelings and have developed much better social and emotional intelligence. However, in their intimate, private life (passive hand) there would still be difficulties. This kind of active-to-passive difference is often found.

Different print patterns are also common, where the prints don't match from active to passive. This is where you find, for instance, a simple arch on the active hand's wall digit and a whorl on the passive palm's wall digit. So as far as outward attitude to life structures is concerned, the person will seek a well-paid, secure job, and will be pragmatic about philosophy and lifestyle. However, at home they might well be fascinated by Buddhism and embrace an alternative lifestyle.

Everything you see on the palm has a positive and a negative side. When you have to explain a negative feature, for instance, the lack of a Life-path Line, you need to explain both pitfalls and benefits. Obviously, the lack of this line shows someone that hasn't come home to themselves and they need to find who they are and what they want. They will not have a clearly defined

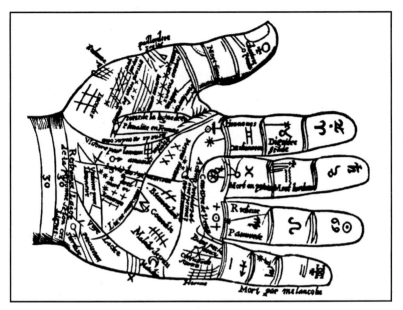

career path. However the benefit of not having this line is that one is completely free to experiment with different lifestyles, job choices and attitudes. It can be liberating to be unformed and to allow yourself to be shaped by experience. Always try to be uplifting and generous in your judgements without skipping the difficult issues you find.

It's quite normal to find contradictions within the palm. Someone may have, for instance, a pair of short mirror fingers and composite prints on both thumbs; this indicates a person lacking in confidence and uncertain as to how to go about getting what they want. Normally this is a recipe for a passive, reflective soul who finds decisions difficult. However, you may well find they have grainy skin, a strong, clear Life-path Line and a strong, straight Line of Consciousness. So this would make for a clear-minded, level-headed, active, successful, business-orientated person who harbours a lot of self-doubt and who consults everyone else before they make a decision. All points have to be added together and put before the person you read for.

People often make huge breakthroughs though having their

palms read. With your help they can suddenly see what's been holding them back and they can find the experience enormously beneficial. A palm reading is like holding up a mirror to someone's soul and showing them how they really are. This is the true magic, power and potential of palm reading, and it's intoxicating.

If you want to take your studies further you may care to work through my other books: 'Palmistry – Apprentice to Pro in 24 Hours' and 'The Spellbinding Power of Palmistry.'

Here's hoping this book has helped you on your own journey into being a palm reader and a liberator of human souls!

Other recommended palmistry books

William Benham
"The Laws of Scientific Hand reading" 1900
reprinted as "The Benham Book of Palmistry" Newcastle 1988

Noel Jaquin
"The Hand Speaks" London 1942

Charlotte Wolff
"The Hand in Psychological Diagnosis" Methuen 1951

Fred Gettings
"The Book of the Hand" Hamlyn 1965
"The Book of Palmistry" Tribune Books 1974
reprinted as "Palmistry" Chancellor Press 1993

Beryl Hutchinson
"Your Life in your hands" Sphere 1967

Frank Clifford 'Palmistry 4 Today'

Schauman & Alter
"Dermatoglyphics in Medical Disorders" Springer 1976

David Brandon-Jones
"Your Palm, Barometer of Health" Rider 1985

Andrew Fitzherbert & Nathaniel Altman
"Palmistry - Your Career in Your Hands" Aquarian 1989

Andrew Fitzherbert
"Hand Psychology" Avery Publishing Group 1989

Bibliography

Brandon-Jones D. 'Your palm, barometer of health' (1985 Rider)

Cummins and Midlo 'Dermatagyphic analysis as diagnostic tool' (Medicine 46, 35 USA) 'Finger prints palms and soles', (1943 New York, Dover publications)'

David T. J. 'The palmer axial triradius, a new method of location' (Human Heredity. 21, 624)

Denton B. 'Principal component analysis of the elongaton of the metacarpal and phalangeal bones' (Am. Jour. Phys Anthropol. Sept 1977)

Greenough, Black and Wallace Experience and brain development. *Child Development, 58*, 539-559. 1987

Hale AR, Phillips JH and Burch GE. 'Features of palmer dermatoglyphics in congenital heart disease' (J.A.M.A. 1176, 41)

'How to build a human' programme BBC2 Sunday 27 Jan 2001

Hummel F. 'Ipsilateral cortical activation of increasing complexity representation' (Clinical Neurophysiology April 2003)

Hutchinson B. 'Your life in your hands' 1967 (Sphere)

Jaquin N. 'The hand speaks' 1942 London

Jones C. 'The interpretation of dermatoglyphic patterns' (1992 Swan Paradise)

Manning J. 'Long ring digit, pointer to autism? (New Scientist March 2001)

Manning J 'Depression index' (9/00 Am. Journ. of Evolution and Behaviour)

Manning J. 'Sex role identity related to ratio of 2nd and 4th digit in women.' (Biological Psychology Feb 2003)

Manning J. 'The ratio of 2nd to 4th digit length and performance in skiing'. (Jour. Sports Med. Phys. Fitness Dec 2002)

Manning J. '2nd to 4th digit ration and offspring sex ratio' (Jour. Theor. Biol. July 2002)

Manning J. 'The ratio of 2nd to 4th digit length – a proxy for testosterone and susceptibility to AIDS?' (Med. Hypotheses Dec 2001)

Napier J. Hands (1980 Allen and Unwin)

Penrose 'Recent advances in human genetics' (LS1965 Churchill).

Putkin B. 'Diagnosis of clubbed fingers' (The lancet GB 9/66)

Raham Q. 'Sexual orientation and the 2nd to 4th finger length ratio: evidence for organising effects of sex hormones or developmental instability?' (Psychoneuro-endocrinology April 2003)

Scheimann E. 'Medical palmistry' (1989 Aquarian)

Shuster C. 'Digital arches in digestive disorder' (8/97 Am. Journal of Gastroenterology)

Wolffe C. 'The hand in psychological diagnosis' (Methuen London)

Dodona Books offers a broad spectrum of divination systems to suit all, including Astrology, Tarot, Runes, Ogham, Palmistry, Dream Interpretation, Scrying, Dowsing, I Ching, Numerology, Angels and Faeries, Tasseomancy and Introspection.